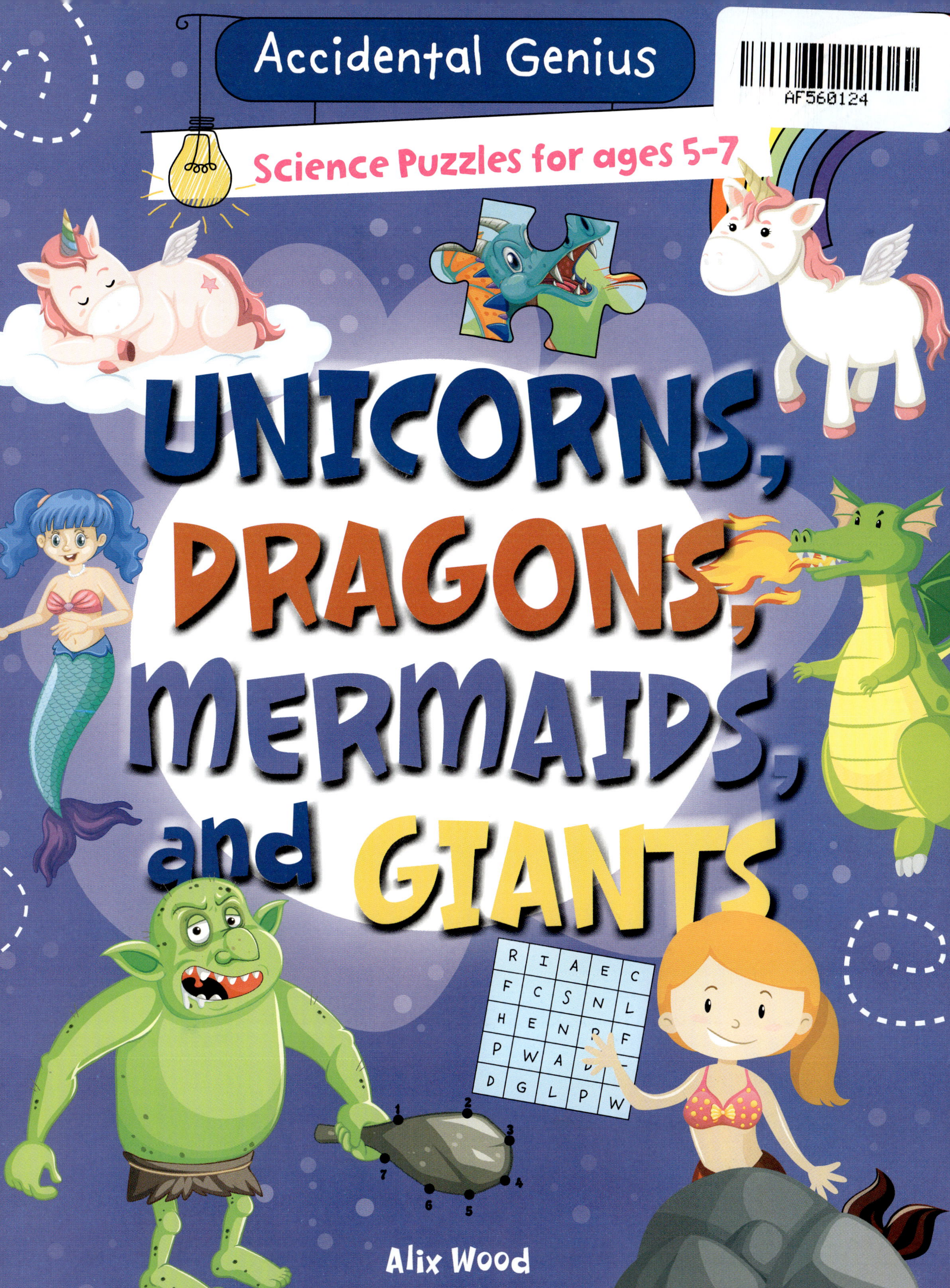
Accidental Genius
Science Puzzles for ages 5-7
UNICORNS, DRAGONS, MERMAIDS, and GIANTS
R I A E C
F C S N L
H E N R F
P W A D
D G L P W
1
2
3
4
5
6
7
Alix Wood

First Published in 2023 by Alix Wood Books



First Edition: 2023

This Reprint Edition: July 2024

Published and Distributed in India by Scholastic India Pvt. Ltd.

ISBN: 978-93-5954-886-9

Written, designed and illustrated by Alix Wood
All other images © AdobeStock Images

Printed in India at Polykam offset New Delhi 110028

# Contents

# Mythical Creatures

Unicorns, fairies, giants, and dragons are all mythical creatures. Myths are stories. Scientists have never found a unicorn or a dragon, so they can't prove if they are real or not!

Long ago, people didn't know enough about science to make sense of everything. If there was a strange rock in the ocean, they might make up a myth about a giant who threw it there!

Can you match each label below to the right mythical creature?

| dragon | unicorn | giant | fairy |
|---|---|---|---|

## Science and Myths

Now, science can usually give us the answers to things that puzzle people. Sometimes, though, myths are proved to be true. In India, there were stories of a city lost under the sea. When a big wave, called a tsunami, pulled the ocean away from the shore, scientists found the sunken buildings! Maybe some other myths are true, too?

Can you find eight mythical creatures in this word search?

GIANT
UNICORN
FAIRY
DRAGON
TROLL
NESSIE
YETI
MERMAID

| | | | | | | | | | |
|---|---|---|---|---|---|---|---|---|---|
| M | W | L | K | T | U | M | Y | N | P |
| D | R | A | G | O | N | L | A | E | M |
| U | G | Q | E | D | I | V | R | S | E |
| P | I | A | M | T | C | R | M | S | H |
| I | A | F | T | E | O | K | N | I | W |
| Y | N | A | U | I | R | L | H | E | V |
| R | T | J | T | Z | N | M | C | Y | D |
| I | W | E | P | H | R | N | A | L | Y |
| A | Y | T | R | O | L | L | U | I | G |
| F | W | Q | E | T | V | E | P | U | D |

# Have You Seen a Unicorn?

If you have, you are very lucky. No scientist has ever seen one! There are other animals people saw and thought were unicorns, though.

Some people thought the one-horned Indian rhinoceros was a unicorn. Its scientific name is *Rhinoceros unicornis*!

## Check the Facts

Unicorns are said to be white, horse-like, and have a long horn on their head. Does that describe the Indian rhinoceros, or the narwhal? Tick the box if the description matches.

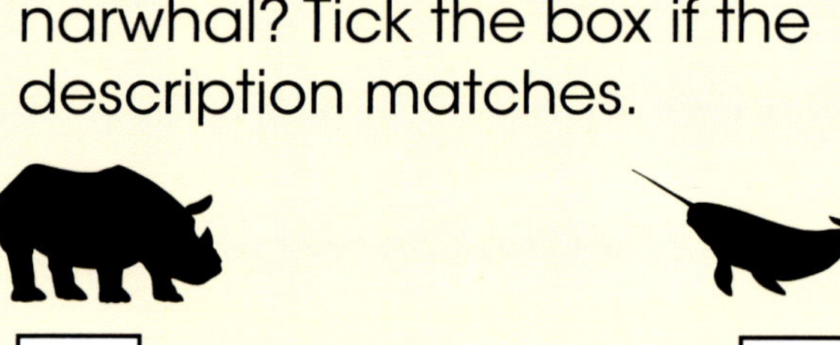

| ☐ | Looks like a horse? | ☐ |
| --- | --- | --- |
| ☐ | Has one horn? | ☐ |
| ☐ | White in color? | ☐ |

A type of whale called a narwhal has one long unicorn-like tusk. It is known as the unicorn of the sea.

Sailors used to bring home narwhal tusks and sell them, pretending they were unicorn horns!

# Color It In

Every year, scientists discover animals no one has seen before. Unicorns are said to be shy, and hide in forests, so maybe someday someone WILL find one!

# Unicorns Long Ago

Did unicorns live a long time ago, and die out, like the dinosaurs? An ancient drawing of a one-horned animal has been found in a cave in France. Is it a unicorn? Or is it a type of bull?

## Join the dots

Do you think this cave drawing looks like a unicorn?

A fossil of an animal found in Asia had one horn coming out of its forehead. Fossils are the remains of plants or animals that lived long ago. Named the Siberian unicorn, scientists think it was really more like a rhinoceros.

## Unicorn Hunt

Can you find 5 unicorns hiding in this picture?

# Colorful Rainbows

Rainbows are so beautiful, it's not surprising people think they are magical. Rainbows happen when the Sun shines through water in the air.

## Make Your Own Magical Rainbow!

**You will need:** a sunny day, an outdoor space, a garden hose attached to a faucet

1. Stand with your back to the Sun.
2. Place your thumb over the end of the hose to create a spray. Watch out, you may get wet!
3. Rainbows show up best against a dark background, such as a hedge or wall.

Did you see a rainbow?

Lights bends and slows down as it passes through water. Light is made up of different colors. Each color of light bends at a different angle – so you see each color separately!

Legend says rainbows point to where a pot of gold is buried! But, did you know rainbows don't have ends? They are really giant circles! From the ground, we can just see half the circle!

## Color It In

1 = red

2 = orange

3 = yellow

4 = green

5 = blue

6 = indigo

7 = violet

1

2

3

4

5

6

7

Unicorns are said to eat rainbows!

# Unicorn Horns

It is said that unicorn horns are spirals. Or, actually, they are helix-shaped. Spirals are flat, two-dimensional shapes. A helix is a three-dimensional spiral.

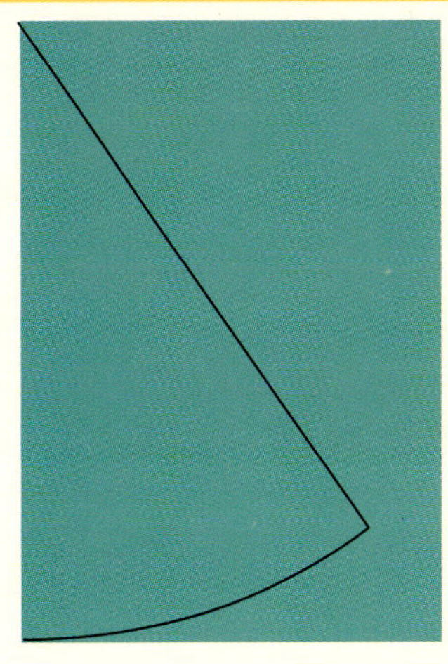

## Make a Unicorn Horn

**You will need:** card stock, pencil, ruler, scissors, yarn, tape.

1. Using a ruler, draw a slanted line from one corner of the card stock. Give the triangle shape a curved bottom.

2. Cut out the shape using scissors. You may want an adult to help you.

3. Roll the triangle into a cone. Leave a small hole at the point. Tape along the cone edge to hold it in place.

4. Poke the yarn through the hole at the top of the cone. Tape the end securely inside the cone.

5. Wrap the other end of the yarn in a spiral around the cone. Secure it with tape at the bottom. Trim off any extra yarn.

6. Tape two more pieces of yarn to the bottom of the cone. Use these to tie the horn to your head.

Sparkly yarn and multi-colored card stock look great, if you have some!

# Gigantic Giants

There are lots of stories about giants. Giants are huge humans. An average man is around 5 feet 9 inches (1.76 m) tall. Giants in stories are usually much bigger, and scary!

We grow when the cells in our bodies get bigger, or split to make more cells. Special chemicals in our bodies tell our cells when to grow, and when to stop growing.

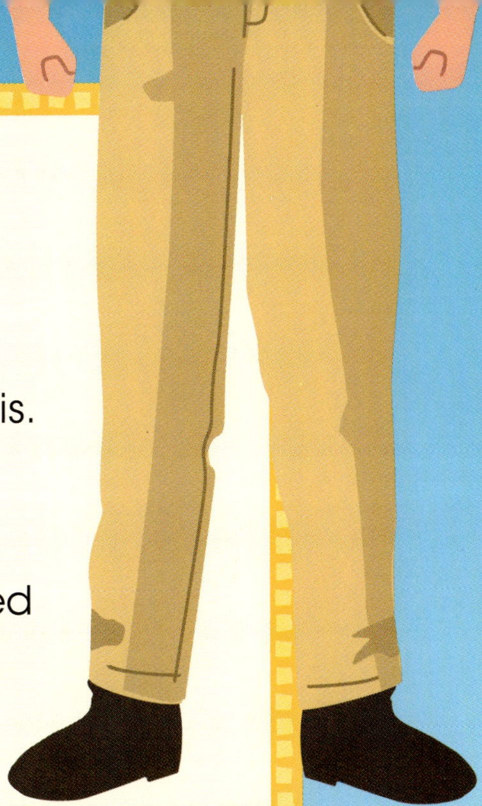

## A Real-life Giant

Born in Alton, Illinois, USA, in 1918, Robert Ludlow was 8 feet 11 inches (2.47 m) tall! Some people called him the Giant of Illinois. At age six he was already 5 feet 7 inches (1.74 m) tall.

Robert had a medical problem that caused him to grow so tall. Now, doctors would be able to cure the problem, so probably no one will ever grow that tall again.

Can you number these men from shortest to tallest? Write 1 under the shortest, up to 6 under the tallest).

# Rock-moving Giants

Have you ever seen a huge rock and wondered how it got there? In Northern Ireland there is a huge group of strange, hexagon-shaped rocks, known as the Giant's Causeway.

The rocks head out into the sea, toward Scotland, like a sunken road. Hexagon-shaped rocks rise up again on the other side of the sea, in Scotland!

## The Story of Finn McCool

Giant Finn McCool wanted to fight the Scottish giant, Benandonner. He built a huge road across the sea to Scotland.

As Benandonner crossed the causeway, Finn saw how big he was! Afraid, Finn disguised himself as his own baby. Benandonner was scared how big the baby was. The baby's father must be even bigger! So he ran back across the causeway to Scotland!

Can you get Benandonner across the Giant's Causeway to Finn McCool?

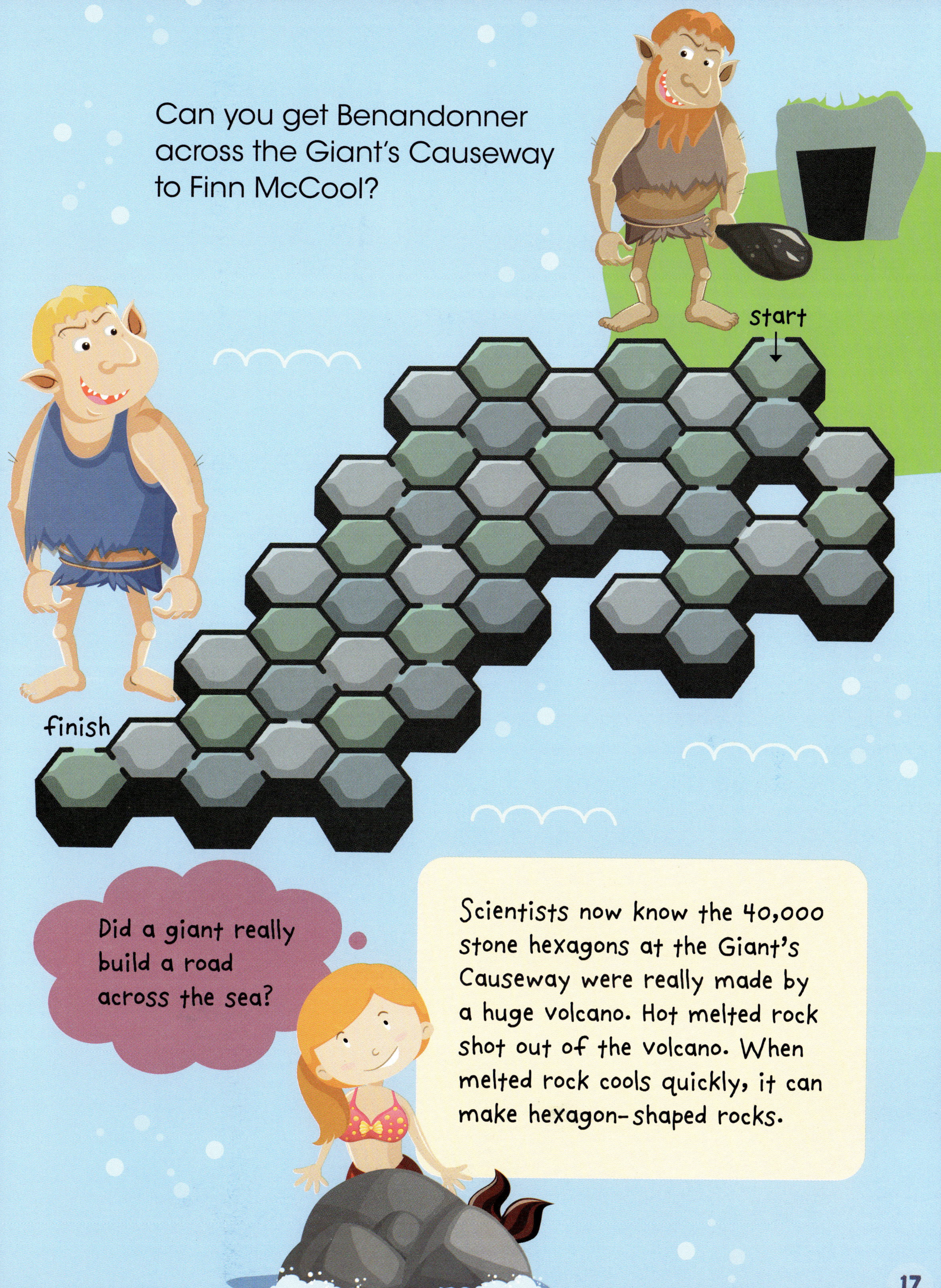


Scientists now know the 40,000 stone hexagons at the Giant's Causeway were really made by a huge volcano. Hot melted rock shot out of the volcano. When melted rock cools quickly, it can make hexagon-shaped rocks.

# Mountain Monsters

The Yeti is said to live in the snowy mountains of Nepal. People who have seen it say it is around 6 foot (1.8 m) tall and covered in hair. It walks on two legs.

## Science and Yetis

Every living thing has DNA. DNA is like a recipe. It holds information about how the living thing is made. Some museums have hair, skin, and teeth that people believe are from a Yeti. Could their DNA prove Yetis are real?

Scientists tested the DNA. The objects were all found to really be from either cows, horses, or bears. Some of the types of bear lived long ago, and may have looked a little like the Yeti, though.

High in the Himalayan Mountains, mountaineers have found strange, wide footprints in the snow. Could they have been made by a Yeti? Follow the lines to see who made these footprints.

Yeti

Bigfoot

A bear

Could the footprints have been made by a hoaxer? A hoaxer is someone who plays tricks on people. Some people have made pretend Yeti tracks in the snow, just for fun!

# Little Mermaids

Have you read any stories about mermaids? Mermaids are said to be half human, with a fish-like tail. They live in water. All mermaids are female. Male mermaids are called Mermen.

Undersea
Search
Find
1 octopus
2 dolphins
3 sea horses
4 jellyfish
5 clownfish
Color It In

# At Home in Water

Mermaids in stories are usually happiest in the sea. It would be hard to walk on land with a fish-like tail! They are friends with all the sea creatures.

## Wordsearch

Can you find the eight sea creatures?

| | | | | | | | | | |
|---|---|---|---|---|---|---|---|---|---|
| U | C | S | J | Z | O | W | Y | H | W |
| M | E | R | M | A | I | D | H | P | H |
| E | S | K | A | T | C | S | R | O | A |
| P | X | C | F | B | I | U | D | N | L |
| F | M | Y | T | F | S | Q | O | U | E |
| G | D | S | R | S | E | A | L | R | L |
| U | P | A | N | C | D | T | P | T | S |
| D | T | I | M | H | Q | N | H | A | O |
| S | J | E | L | L | Y | F | I | S | H |
| L | O | B | S | T | E | R | N | R | S |

CRAB
JELLYFISH
DOLPHIN
STARFISH
MERMAID
WHALE
LOBSTER
SEAL

Mermaids love to float in the water. Why do some things float and others sink? It depends on their density. Density is how tightly packed the material inside an object is.

Being heavy does not always mean a thing will sink. Ships are heavy, but their shape causes air to be trapped inside them. Air is less dense than water, so they float.

## Float or Sink?

Circle the things that will float in water.

Does a lemon sink or float? That depends! With the skin on, it floats. Take the skin off, and it sinks. Why? The skin traps air around the lemon, and keeps it from soaking up water.

# Sea Monsters

A huge monster squid is believed to live in the sea around Norway. Stories tell of it dragging ships under the water with its powerful arms. If that failed, it would swim around the ship in circles. The whirlpool it created would pull the ship under.

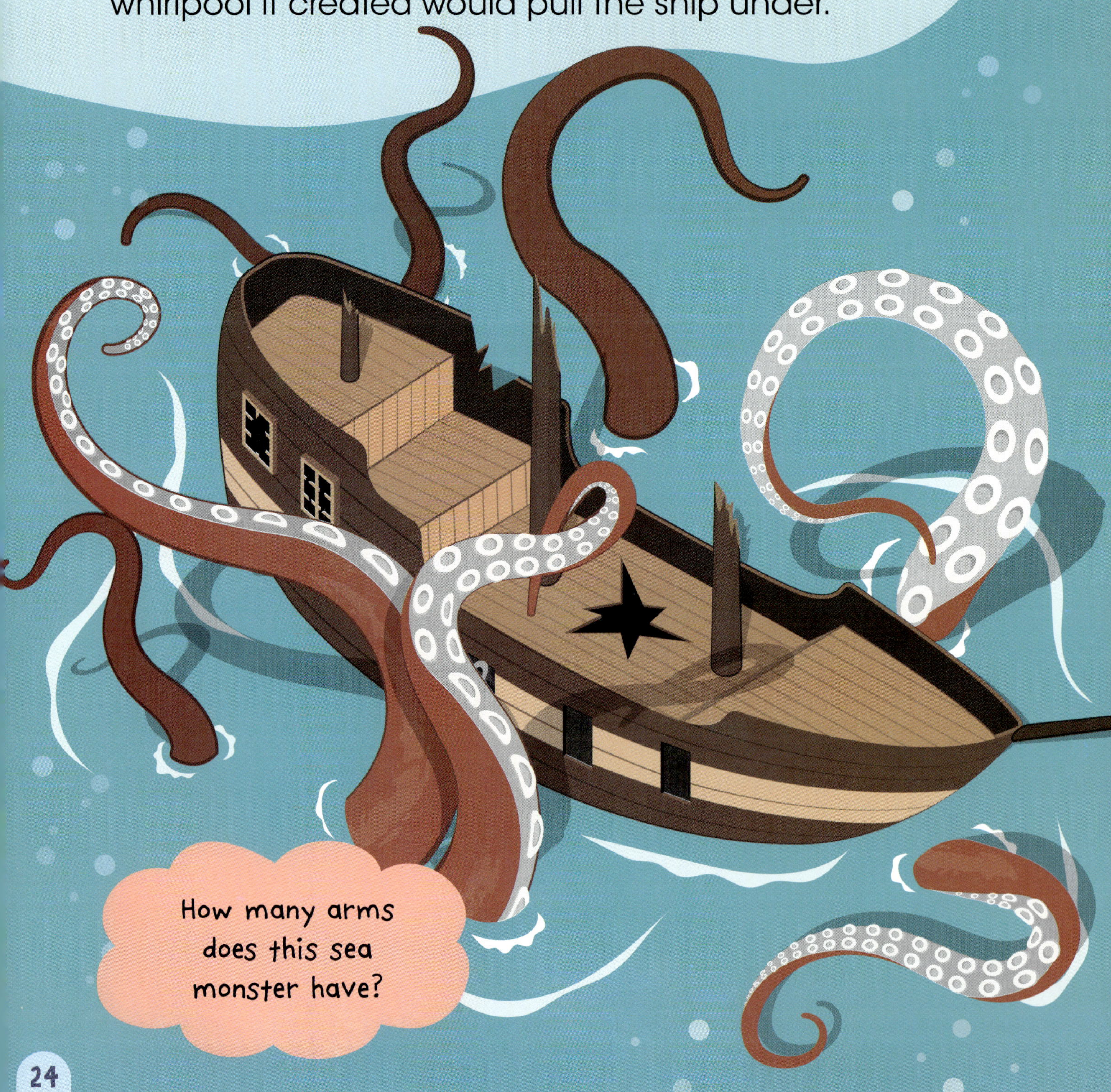

## Create a Whirlpool

**You will need:** two empty plastic water bottles, duct tape, water

1. Fill one bottle three-quarter full of water.
2. With the bottle openings together, tightly tape the empty bottle to the top of the other bottle.
3. Turn the bottles over, so the one with water is on top. Hold the top bottle and swirl it in a tight circle. Then place the bottles on a table and watch the whirlpool.

How does a whirlpool sink a ship? As the water starts to spin, it pushes outward and leaves a hole in the middle. A ship can then fall into the hole!

## Crossout Puzzle

Cross out any letters that appear twice in this grid. Write each letter that only appears once in a circle. Then unscramble the letters to find the name of a real sea creature that can grow very big.

| | | | | |
|---|---|---|---|---|
| T | A | G | D | F |
| H | W | T | R | Q |
| F | S | A | N | G |
| I | R | M | W | P |
| P | N | U | H | M |

# The Loch Ness Monster

For hundreds of years, people have reported seeing a monster at a deep, Scottish lake called Loch Ness. The creature, known as Nessie, has a long neck that sticks out of the water.

At dusk you might only see the outline of Nessie against the evening sky. Which of these silhouettes matches Nessie?

Scientists have searched Loch Ness. It is hard to find a creature in such a big, deep lake. They use sonar.

Sonar sends sound waves underwater. The sound waves bounce off solid objects. Scientists can create a picture of objects under the water. Up to now, they haven't found Nessie!

Can you find Nessie on the busy loch?

# Magical Fairies

Fairies in stories are said to look like tiny humans. They fly, either using wings, or using magic. They have magical powers and can make potions and grant wishes. Fairies can be naughty, or nice!

## Make a Magic Potion

**You will need:** baking soda, vinegar, dish soap, food coloring or powder paint, a small jar, a sink or bath tub, a spoon

1. In a sink or bath tub, half-fill the jar with vinegar.

2. Mix in some powder paint or food coloring.

3. Add a squeeze of dish soap and a spoonful of baking soda. Watch as your potion bubbles up over the top of the jar!

What's happening? Mixing baking soda and vinegar creates a chemical reaction. The reaction causes bubbles of carbon dioxide gas. The dish soap turns the bubbles into a foam.

# Color It In

# Scary Dragons

Have you read any stories about dragons? They are usually quite scary, with scaly skin, wings. And, they breathe fire!

Draw a line to match the label to the correct part of the dragon.

If you are sharing this book, cover the dragon with tracing paper, then draw your lines.

Are there real fire-breathing, flying dragons? Draco lizards can fly. They don't have wings. They glide using flaps of skin on either side of their body. Draco is another word for dragon! A giant lizard called the Komodo dragon can grow to 10 feet (3 m) long! But neither of these lizards breathe fire!

## Dragon Jigsaw

Can you find the missing pieces to finish this dragon jigsaw?

# Dragon Homes

Dragons live in castles, forests, and caves in stories. Can you match each dragon to their description? And then, match each dragon to the right home? Use a different color pencil for each dragon.

This dragon has wings. He uses them to fly to his luxury castle on the hill.

This dragon has horns. They help him burrow into the rock in his cave.

This dragon has a spiny tail. She uses it to balance when she hides up in the trees.

## Breathing Fire

Could an animal really breathe fire? The bombardier beetle sets off a small chemical explosion if it is scared. Boiling hot chemicals shoot out from its abdomen! So, maybe a dragon could shoot out a gas that gets set on fire?

boiling hot gas

# Will-o'-the-Wisp

It is said a bad fairy called Will-o'-the-Wisp leads people into muddy swamps at night! He is also known as Jack-o'-Lantern. The fairy creates wispy lights over the swamp. People follow the lights and get stuck in the mud.

In a folk story, a man named Jack tricked the devil. When Jack died, he wasn't allowed in heaven, or hell. The devil felt sorry for him. He gave him some coal to light his turnip lantern. Now, with nowhere to go, the ghostly fairy and his lantern wanders the swamp.

### What are the wispy lights really?

When plants rot in a swamp they produce a gas. The gas makes a flickering light.

Copy the drawing in each square into the correct square in the grid below. What did you draw?

What day of the year might you see a Jack-o'-Lantern?

# Rocky Trolls

A troll is an ugly, unfriendly monster from Northern Europe. Rocks around the coast of Iceland are said to have once been trolls! People believed trolls turned to stone if they went out in daylight. It was a fun way of explaining strange-looking rocks in the sea!

This troll-shaped rock in Iceland was formed by erosion. Erosion is when natural forces, such as waves, move rock from one place to another.

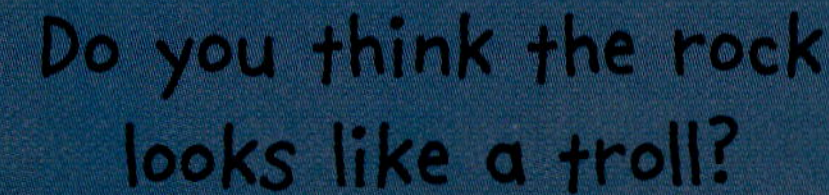

## The Power of Water

**You will need:** mud, pebbles, an outdoor space, water and a watering can

Do you think water could move rock? Try this experiment. Go outside and make a small hill using mud and pebbles. Then pour water on your hill. What happens? The water will probably break up the mud and move the pebbles. That's erosion!

## Shape Match

Can you match the silhouette to the right troll?

# Angry Trolls

Trolls are nasty, but not very clever. There is a fairy tale about a troll who lived under a bridge. Little Billy Goat, Middle-sized Billy Goat, and Big Billy Goat wanted to cross the bridge to find fresh grass to eat. But the troll wanted to eat them!

The angry troll tore up the story!

Can you match the right page to each picture on page 39?

As Little Billy Goat's hooves went *trip trap* across the bridge, the angry troll came out.

Little Billy Goat squeaked "Don't eat ME! My brother is on his way and he is much bigger and tastier!"

1

Then Middle-sized Billy Goat went *trip trap* across the bridge. The hungry troll came out.

Middle-sized Billy Goat trembled "Don't eat ME! My brother is on his way. He is much bigger and tastier!"

2

As Big Billy Goat's hooves went *trip trap* across the bridge, the starving troll came out.

Big Billy Goat yelled "You're not eating me!" He charged at the troll and tossed him into the water. The troll was never seen again.

3

## Can You Build a Bridge from Paper?

**You will need:** two thick books, paper, some coins

Cut a strip of paper around 3 inches (7.5 cm) wide. Lay it across the two books. How many coins can you place on it before it collapses? Next, fold up both long sides, to make a U-shape. Now how many coins will your bridge hold?

The U-shape folds makes the bridge much stronger.

# How Do Dragons Fly?

Some dragons in stories fly, and others don't. Could a big, heavy dragon really fly? Maybe, if they were built the right way.

Bones are heavy. Flying dinosaurs, birds, and bats have hollow bones. This makes their bones lighter.

Dragons would need big wings. Large flying dinosaurs had very big wings.

One flying dinosaur had air-sacs in its body. They filled with gas, like a balloon. Fish have air-sacs that help them float.

A short tail is best. A long tail creates drag. Drag is when air hits an object and slows it down.

Having just two legs would help a dragon fly. Birds and bats have two wings and two legs. So did the flying dinosaurs.

Which dragon is most likely to be able to fly?

Join the dots to help this dragon fly.

# What Would They Eat?

To figure out what a mythical creature eats, a scientist would decide what animal they were most like. And then make what is known as an educated guess. The mythical creature would probably eat the same food.

If an animal only eats meat it is called a carnivore. Animals that only eat plants are called herbivores. An animal that eats both meat and plants is an omnivore.

Can you match the right word with the right mythical creature?

# Mythical Creature Genius Test

Are you a mythical creature genius? Answer these questions to find out.

1 What is a myth?

a) A flying insect.

b) A monster that lives in the mountains.

c) An untrue story that tries to explain the world around us.

2 Which of these animals might have been mistaken for a unicorn?

a) an elephant b) a rhinoceros c) a hippopotamus

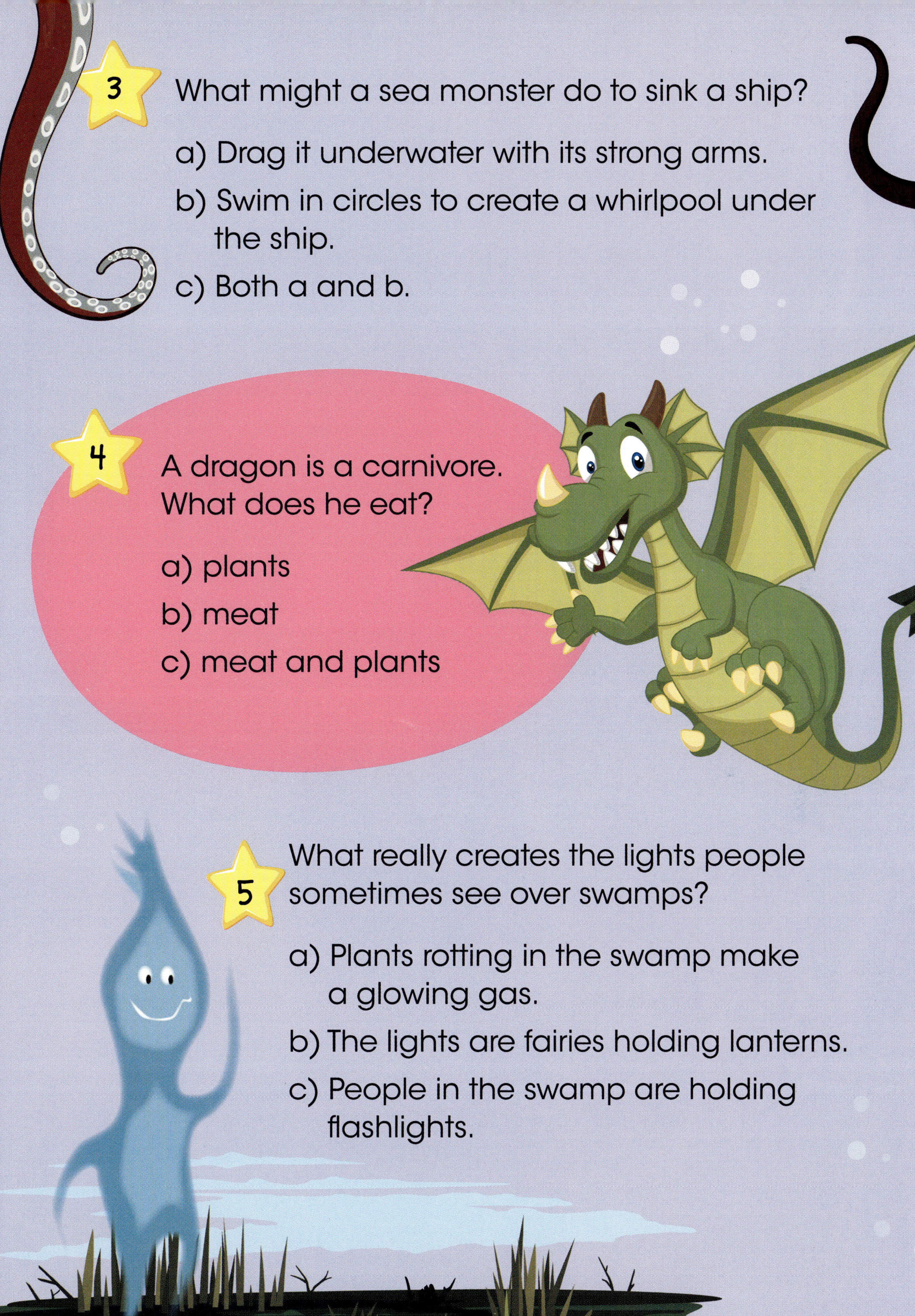

3 What might a sea monster do to sink a ship?

a) Drag it underwater with its strong arms.
b) Swim in circles to create a whirlpool under the ship.
c) Both a and b.

4 A dragon is a carnivore. What does he eat?

a) plants
b) meat
c) meat and plants

5 What really creates the lights people sometimes see over swamps?

a) Plants rotting in the swamp make a glowing gas.
b) The lights are fairies holding lanterns.
c) People in the swamp are holding flashlights.

# Answers

Page 4:

Page 5:

| | | | | | | | | | |
|---|---|---|---|---|---|---|---|---|---|
| M | W | L | K | T | U | M | Y | N | P |
| D | R | A | G | O | N | L | A | E | M |
| U | G | Q | E | D | I | V | R | S | E |
| P | I | A | M | T | C | R | M | S | H |
| I | A | F | T | E | O | K | N | I | W |
| Y | N | A | U | I | R | L | H | E | V |
| R | T | J | T | Z | N | M | C | Y | D |
| I | W | E | P | H | R | N | A | L | Y |
| A | Y | T | R | O | L | L | U | I | G |
| F | W | Q | E | T | V | E | P | U | D |

Page 6:

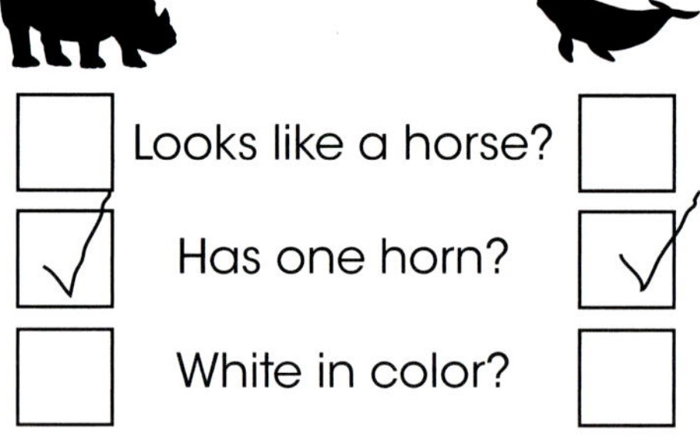


Page 8: scientists think the cave drawing is a type of bull.

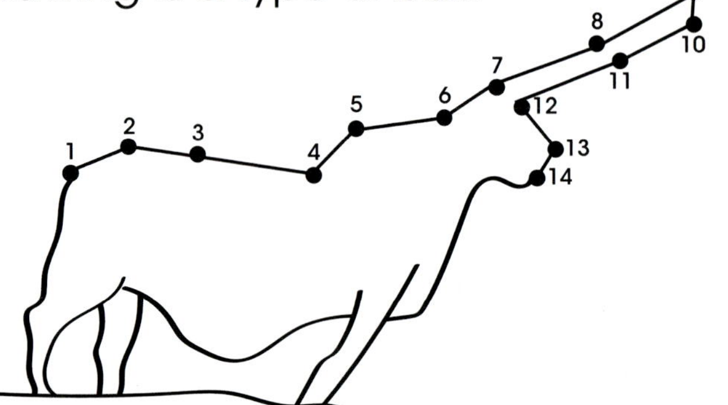

Page 9:

Page 11:

Page 15:

Page 17:

Page 19:

Page 20: as a mermaid is like a human, they probably breathe using lungs.

Page 21:

Page 22:

| | | | | | | | | | |
|---|---|---|---|---|---|---|---|---|---|
| U | C | S | J | Z | O | W | Y | H | W |
| M | E | R | M | A | I | D | H | P | H |
| E | S | K | A | T | C | S | R | O | A |
| P | X | C | F | B | I | U | D | N | L |
| F | M | Y | T | F | S | Q | O | U | E |
| G | D | S | R | S | E | A | L | R | L |
| U | P | A | N | C | D | T | P | T | S |
| D | T | I | M | H | Q | N | H | A | O |
| S | J | E | L | L | Y | F | I | S | H |
| L | O | B | S | T | E | R | N | R | S |

Page 23:

Page 25: The crossout puzzle word is SQUID.

Page 26: a

Page 27:

Page 30:

Page 31: a) 4; b) 3; c) 1; d) 2

Page 32:

Page 34:

Page 37: 1) b; 2) a; 3) d; 4) c

Page 38-39: 1) C; 2) B; 3) A

Page 41 top: c is most likely to be able to fly. He has two legs, big wings and a smallish tail.

Page 41 bottom:

Page 43:

Page 44: 1) c - a myth is an untrue story that tries to explain the world around us 2) b - a rhinoceros has been mistaken for a unicorn 3) c - both a and b 4) b - carnivores eat meat 5) a - plants rotting in the swamp make a glowing gas